CHRIS K
W9-CBU-702

LEVEL 1

PIANO Adventures®

by Nancy and Randall Faber

THE BASIC PIANO METHOD

CONTENTS

Stuffing the Stockings (interval review) 3

Angels We Have Heard on High 4
Christmas Stocking Stuffers 5

Up on the Housetop 6
Chimney Stocking Stuffers 7

We Three Kings of Orient Are 8
Starry Stocking Stuffers 9

Deck the Halls 10
Fa la la Stocking Stuffers 11

O Come, All Ye Faithful 12
Joyful Stocking Stuffers 13

O Come, Little Children 14
Children's Stocking Stuffers 15

Jingle Bells 16
Sleighbell Stocking Stuffers 19

Christmas Music Calendar 20

About the "Sightreading Stocking Stuffers"

A student's enthusiasm for learning Christmas music can become an opportunity to create enthusiasm for sightreading. In this book, each Christmas song is presented with short melodies, called "Sightreading Stocking Stuffers."

The "Sightreading Stocking Stuffers" are **melodic variations** of the carol being studied. Teachers will notice that the lyrics and rhythm patterns are from the carol. By drawing on these familiar rhythms, the student may effectively focus on interval reading and note reading.

The student should sightread one "stocking stuffer" a day while learning the Christmas song. Or, the stocking stuffers can be used as sightreading during the lesson itself.

The teacher may wish to tell the student:

> **Sightreading means "reading music at first sight."**
>
> When sightreading, music is not practiced over and over. Instead, it is only played once or twice with the highest concentration.

The following **3 C's** may help the student with sightreading:

C **CORRECT HAND POSITION**
Find the correct starting note for each hand.

C **COUNT - OFF**
Set a steady tempo by counting one "free" measure before starting to play.

C **CONCENTRATE**
Focus your eyes on the music, carefully reading the intervals.

Note to Teacher: This page reviews intervals and prepares the student for the carols and sightreading that follow.

Stuffing the Stockings

Each musical "gift" is an interval: **2nd**, **3rd**, **4th**, or **5th**.
Draw a line connecting each "gift" to the correct stocking.

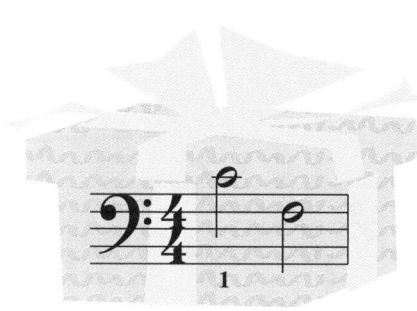

Extra Credit: Play each "gift" on the piano using the fingering given.

Angels We Have Heard on High

Traditional

Quickly, with joy

3 *on* ___?

f An - gels we have heard on high,
And the moun - tains in re - ply,

1 *on* ___?
5 *on* ___?

5 13

mf sweet - ly sing - ing o'er the plains,
ech - o - ing their joy - ous strains.

repeat!

17 29

21 33

f Glo - - - - - - - - - - -

L.H. 2 *over*

(Return L.H. to C Position)

Teacher Duet: (Student plays *1 octave higher*)

R.H.

L.H. *p*

17 29

mp

21 33

25 37

cresc.

mf

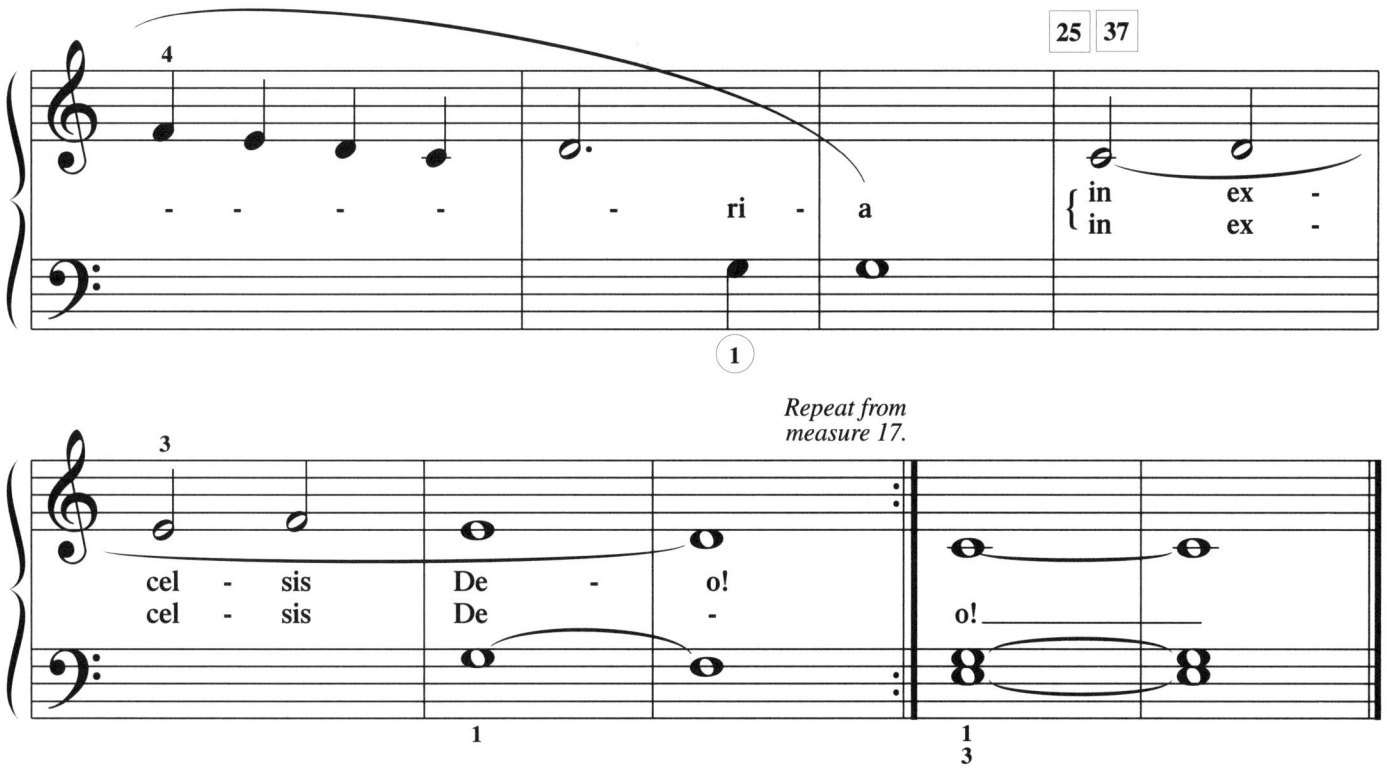

Sightread one "stocking stuffer" a day while you are learning the carol. The words to the "stocking stuffers" are familiar, but the **melodies have changed!**

Circle the stocking after sightreading!

("variations" for sightreading)

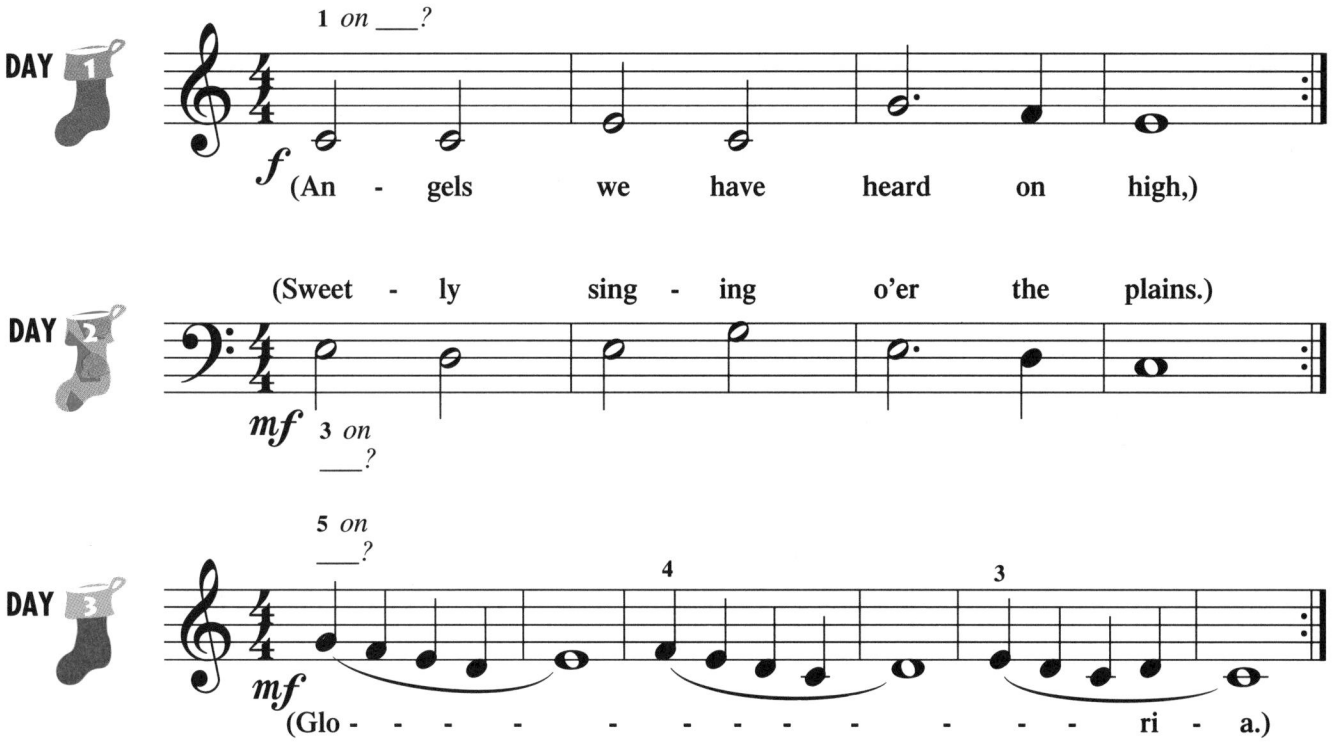

Can you find the melody of **Day 2** in the carol? Hint: It is in the treble clef.

Can you sing from measure 17 to the end of the carol?

Up on the Housetop

Words and Music by
Benjamin R. Hanby

Lively

2 *on* ___?

mf Up on the house - top rein - deer pause,
Down through the chim - ney (with) lots of toys,

2 *on* ___?

5 13

out jumps good old San - ta Claus.
all for little ones' Christ - mas joys.

1. First Time Only :) 2.

17 21

f Ho, ho, ho! Who would - n't go! Ho, ho, ho!

p *f*

(prepare) (prepare)

Teacher Duet: (Student plays *1 octave higher*)

R.H.

L.H.

p 5 13 1. 2. 17 21 *mf* *mf* 25 29 *p* *sub.* *p* *mf*

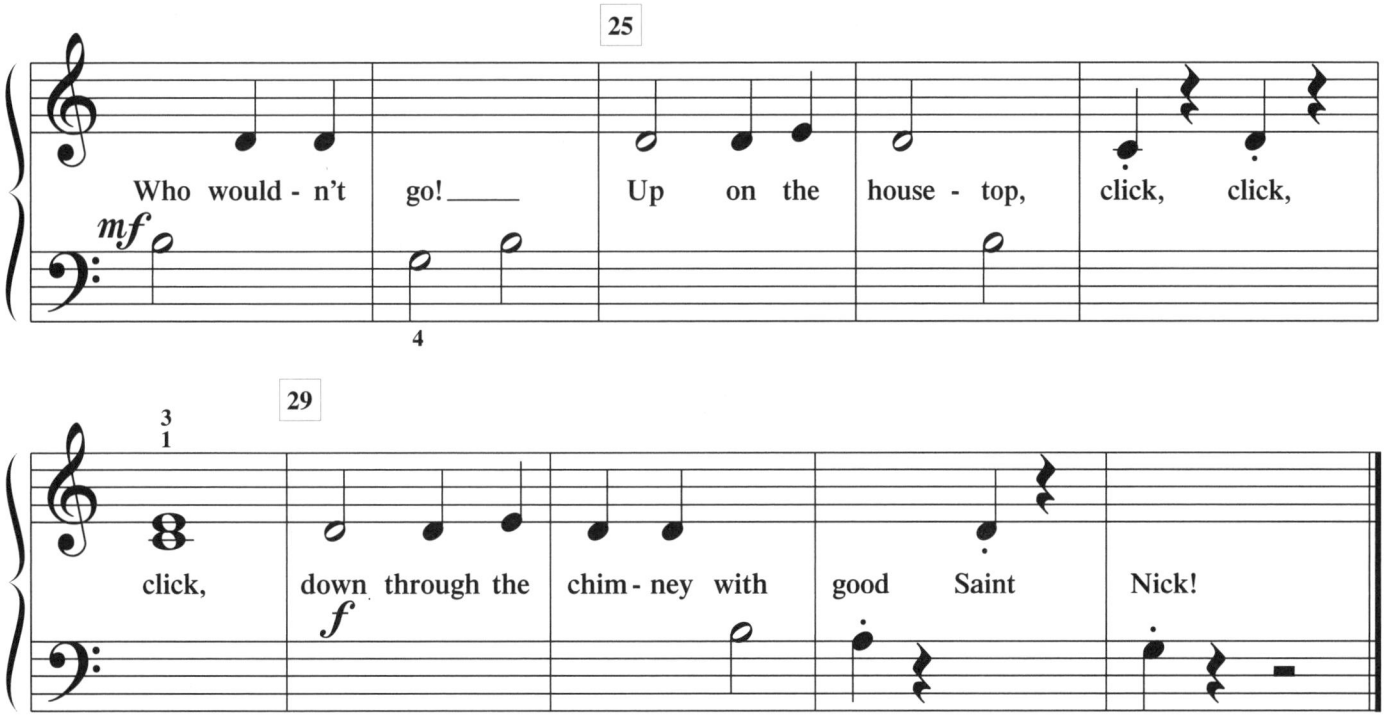

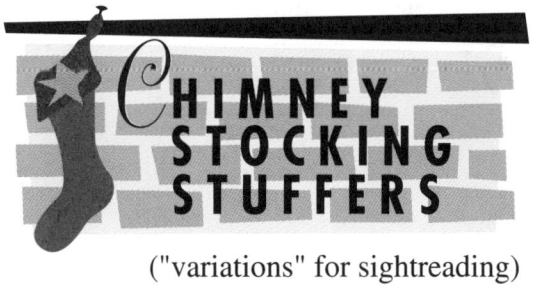

("variations" for sightreading)

Sightread one "stocking stuffer" a day while learning *Up on the Housetop.*

Circle the stocking after sightreading!

DAY 1

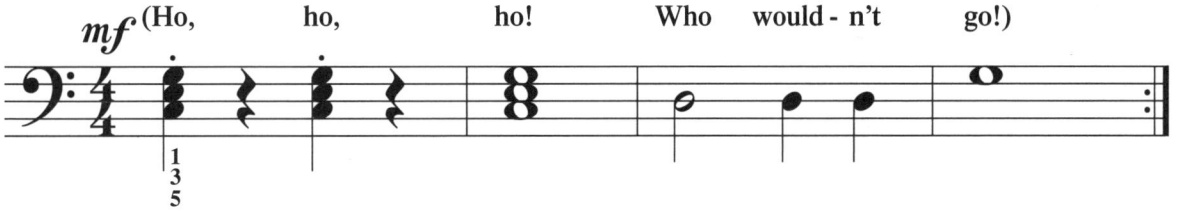

DAY 2

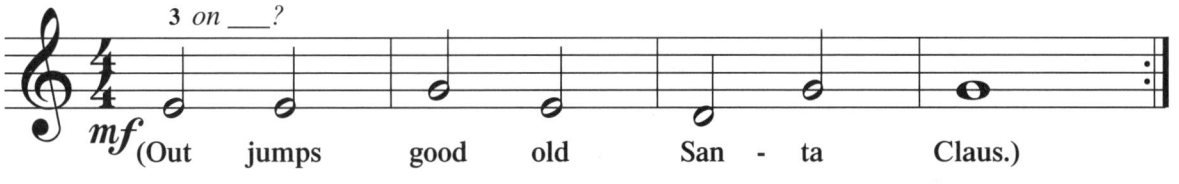

DAY 3

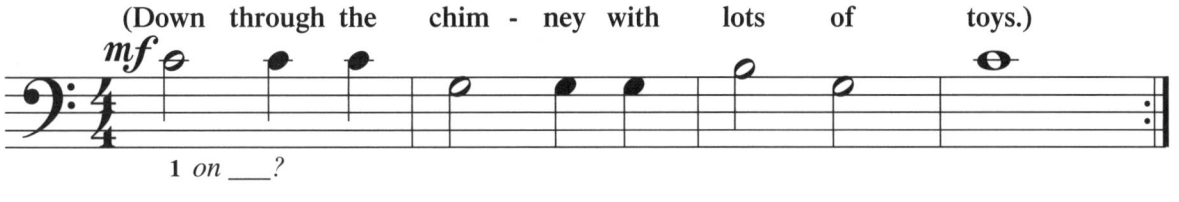

DAY 4

Circle all the **4ths** in the "stocking stuffers" above.

DAY 5

In *Up on the Housetop,* put a ✔ above each measure with this rhythm:

Hint: There are 5 measures.

We Three Kings of Orient Are

Words and Music by
J.H. Hopkins, Jr.

Flowing smoothly

3 *on* ___?

repeat!

mf We three kings of O - ri - ent are
bear - ing gifts, we trav - erse a - far.

3 *on* ___?

9

Field and foun - tain, moor and moun - tain, fol - low - ing

13

yon - der star. Oh, _____

18 22

1

Star of won - der,
f Star of roy - al

Teacher Duet: (Student plays *1 octave higher*)

1. 2.

9

R.H.

L.H. *p* *with pedal*

13

18 22

mf

26

mp

30

mf

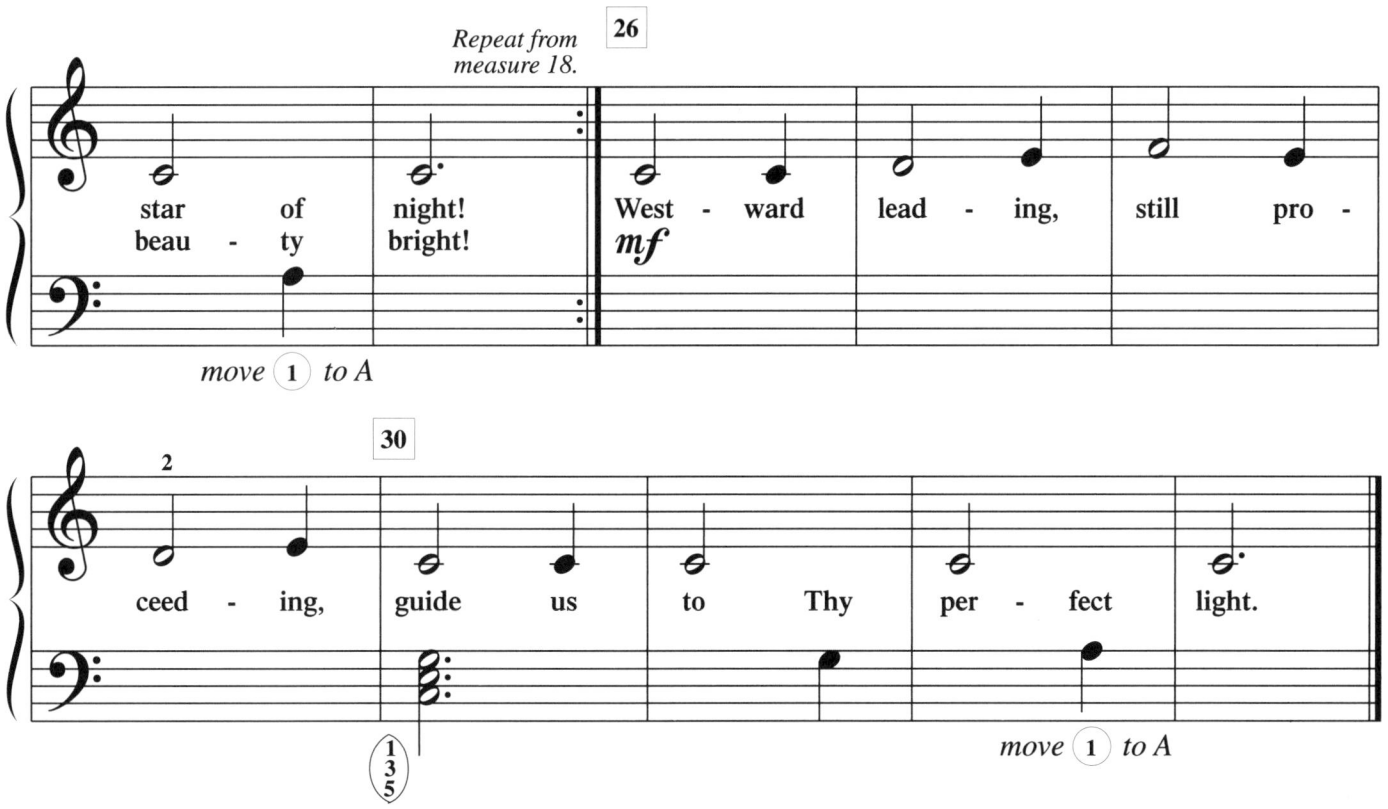

Sightread one "stocking stuffer" a day while learning *We Three Kings of Orient Are.*

Circle the stocking after sightreading!

("variations" for sightreading)

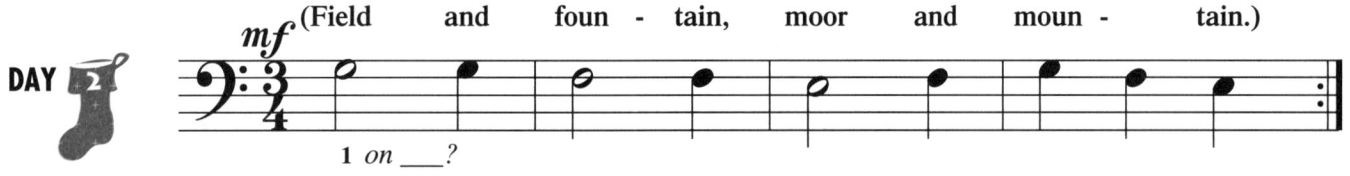

Write the counts "1 - 2 - 3" under the beats for **Day 3.**

Circle the most common rhythm in *We Three Kings of Orient Are.*

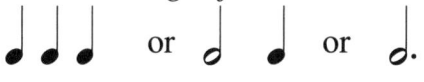

Deck the Halls

Merrily **Traditional**

5 *on* ___?

Deck the halls with boughs of hol - ly,
mf 'Tis the sea - son to be jol - ly,

5 13 *repeat!*

Fa la la la la, la la la la.

(prepare L.H.)

move 1 *to B!*

17 21

Don we now our gay ap - par - el,
mp

grow louder
Fa la la
lift!

Teacher Duet: (Student plays *1 octave higher*)

R.H.

L.H.

mf *mp* *p* *mf* *rit.*

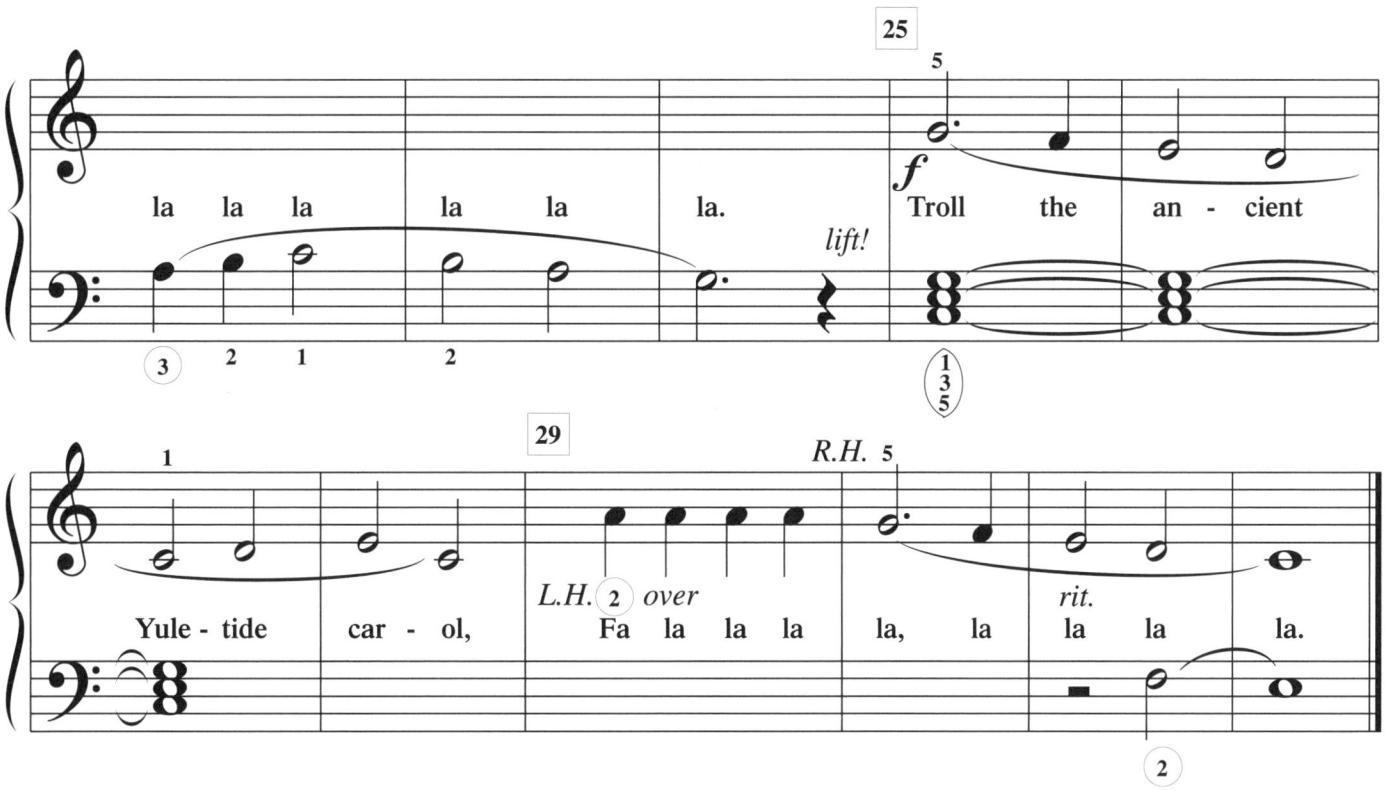

Sightread one "stocking stuffer" a day while learning *Deck the Halls.*

Circle the stocking after sightreading!

("variations" for sightreading)

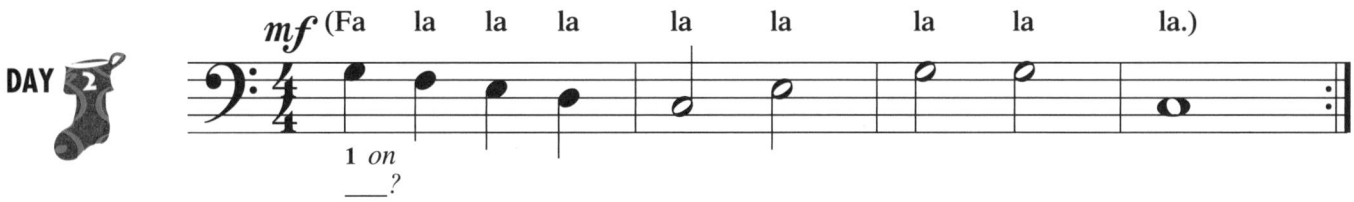

Circle all the **5ths** in the "stocking stuffers" above.

Circle this rhythm each time it appears in *Deck the Halls.*

Hint: It occurs 6 times.

Teacher Note: Some students may wish to substitute the ♩. ♪ rhythm in measures 7, 12, and 19.

O Come, All Ye Faithful

(Adeste Fideles)

Moderately

Transcribed by F. Oakeley
Wade's *"Cantus Diversi"*

1 *on* ___?

mf O come, all ye faith - ful, joy - ful and tri - um - phant, O

3 *on* ___?

5

come ye, O come___ ye to Beth - le - hem. *lift!*

9

5 4 *softly!*

Come and be - hold Him, born the King of an - gels. O

p

(prepare L.H.)

1 3 5 1 4 1

Teacher Duet: (Student plays *1 octave higher*)

R.H.

L.H.

mf

5 9 13 17

p *mp* *cresc.* *mf*

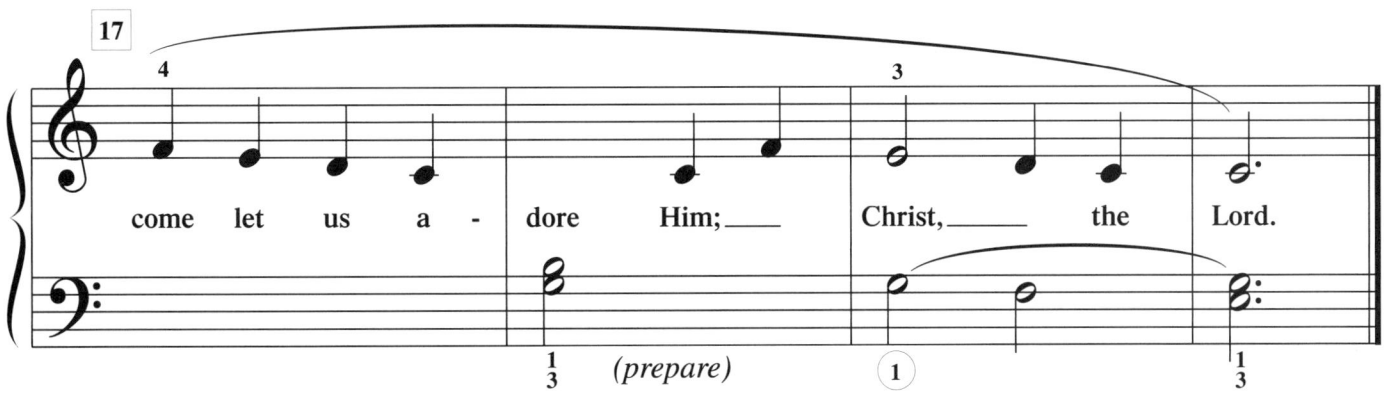

Sightread one "stocking stuffer" a day while learning *O Come, All Ye Faithful.*

Circle the stocking after sightreading!

("variations" for sightreading)

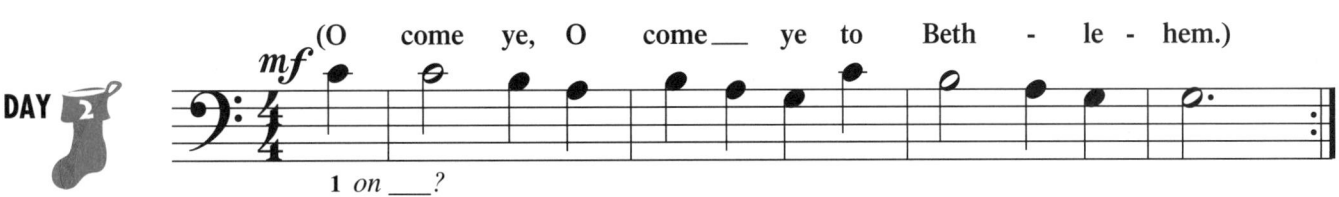

Circle a C chord in the carol.

Circle and label a **2nd**, a **3rd**, a **4th**, and a **5th** in the "stocking stuffers" above.

O Come, Little Children

Words and Music by
Christoph von Schmidt and J.A.P. Schulz

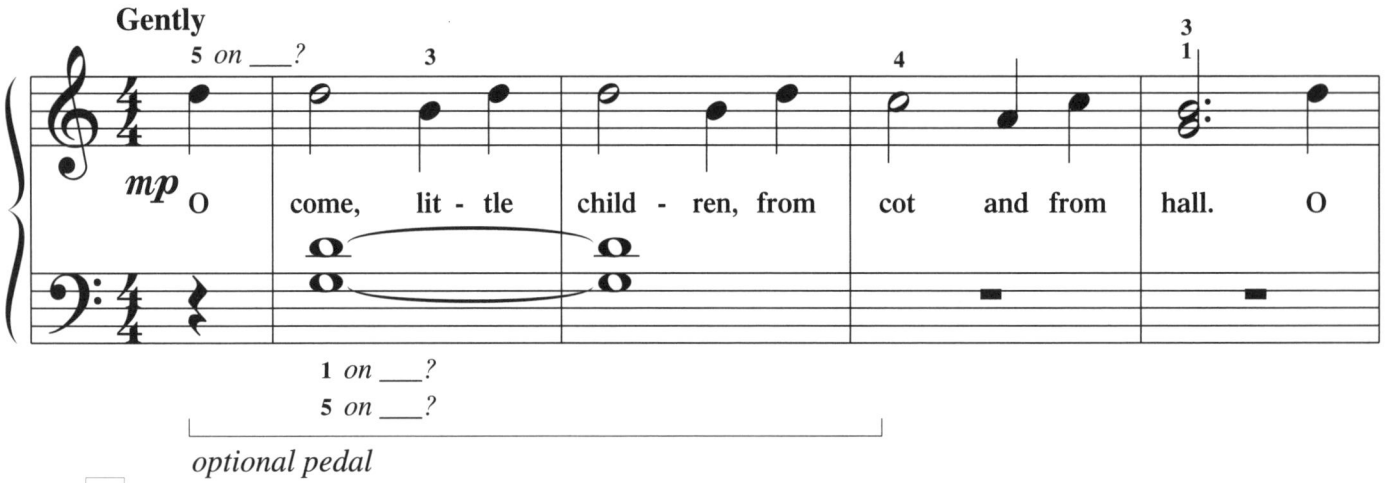

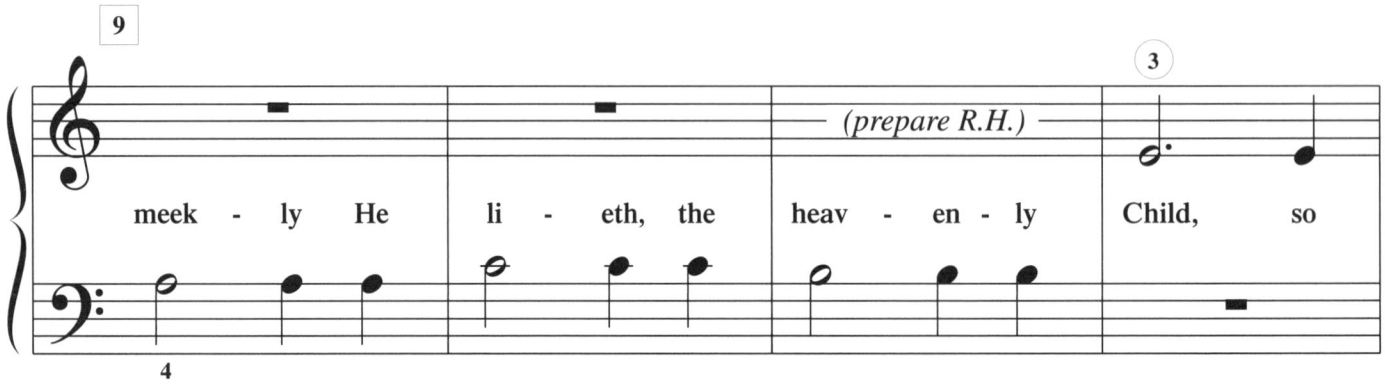

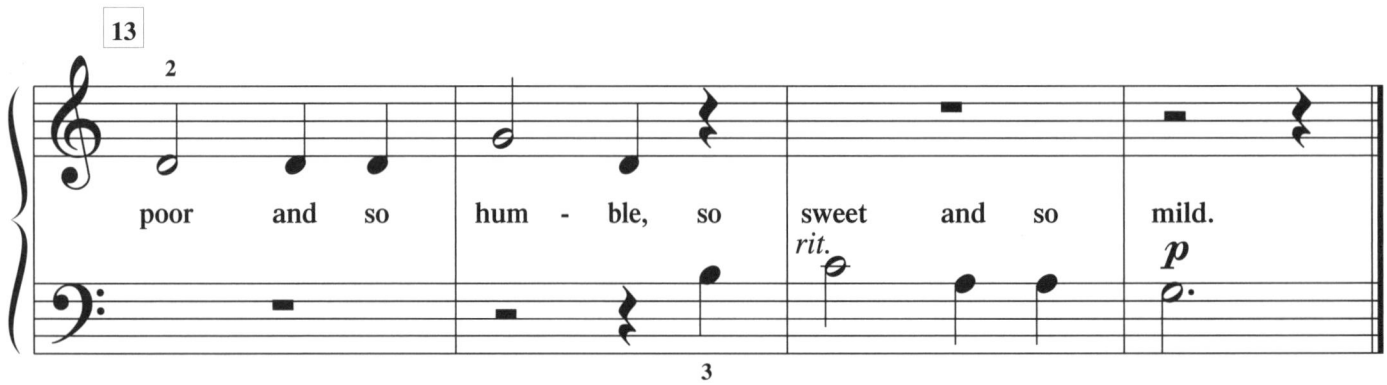

Note: Teacher duet is at the bottom of page 15.

("variations" for sightreading)

Sightread one "stocking stuffer" a day while learning *O Come, Little Children.*

Circle the stocking after sightreading!

DAY 1

DAY 2

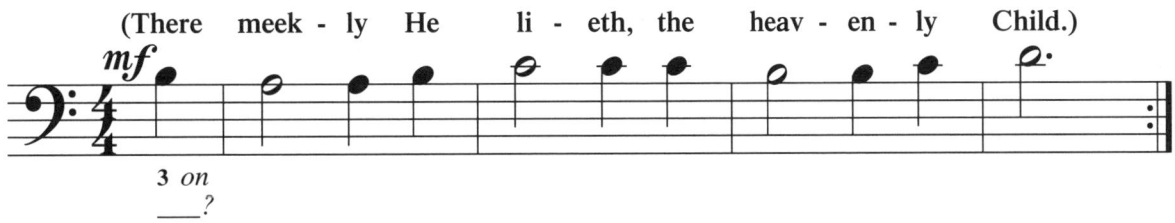

DAY 3

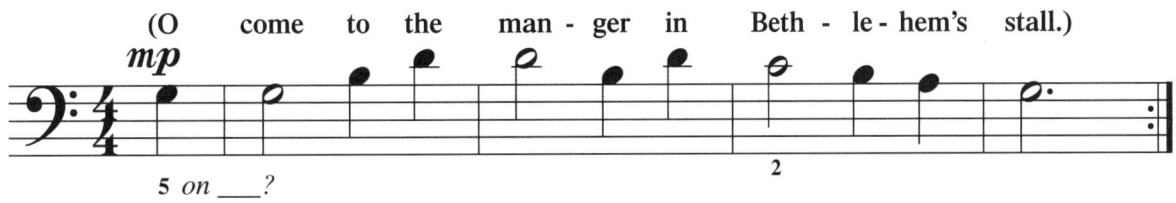

DAY 4

Write the letter names beside each note for **Day 1.**

DAY 5

In *O Come, Little Children,* put a ✔ above each measure with this rhythm:

Hint: There are 12.

Teacher Duet for *O Come, Little Children:* (Student plays *as written.*)

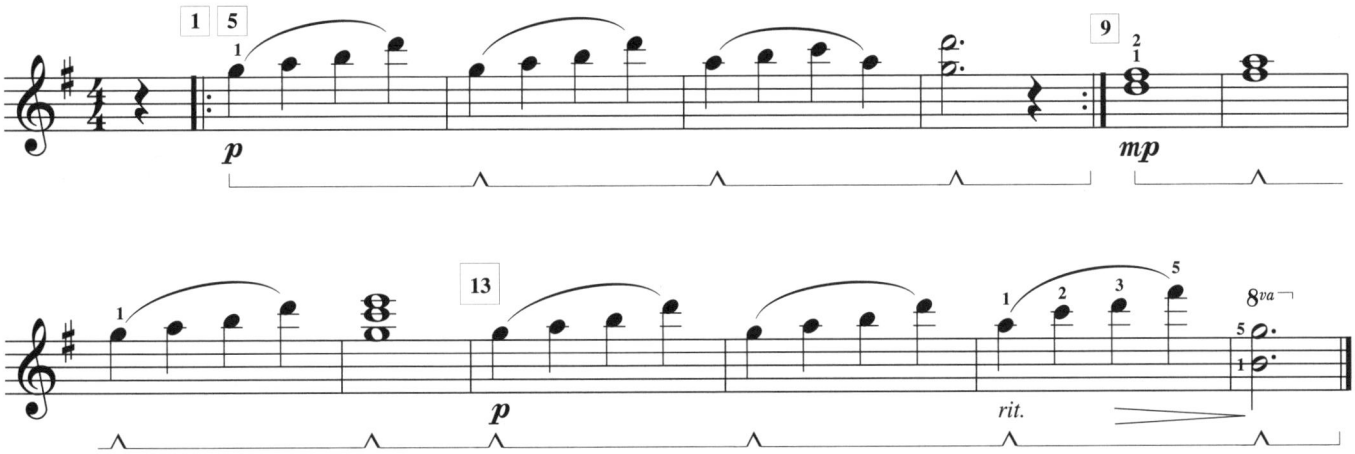

Jingle Bells

Words and Music by
J. Pierpont

Lively

3 *on* ___?

Dash - ing thru the snow in (a) one - horse o - pen sleigh;

mf

5

4 *on* ___?

O'er the fields we go, laugh - ing all the way.

9

Bells on bob - tail ring, mak - ing spir - its bright; What

13

Cross L.H. over 2

5 4 2

fun it is to ride and sing a sleigh - ing song to - night! Oh!

Teacher Duet: (Student plays *1 octave higher*)

1 9

R.H.

L.H. 1 *p*

5 13

1. 2.

For piano solo: Continue on to page 18 for more "Jingle Bell" fun!
For duet: End at measure 32.

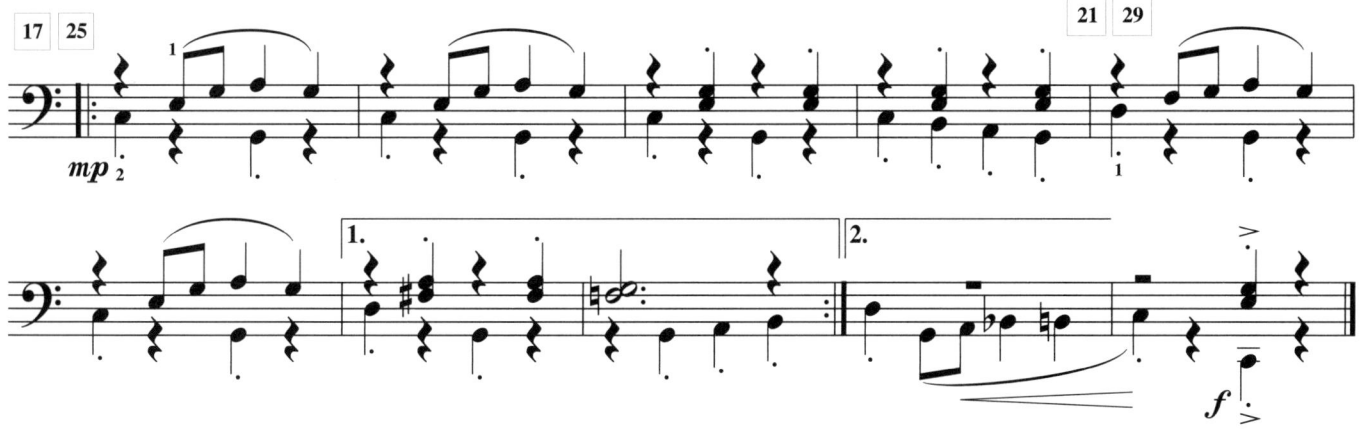

33
(1 - 2 - 3 - 4)
f
(1 - 2 - 3 - 4)
grow softer
mp
37
Jin - gle bells,
p
jin - gle bells,
jin - gle all the way;
41
Oh, what fun it
is to ride in(a) one - horse o - pen sleigh!
grow louder
45
Jin - gle bells,
f
jin - gle bells,
jin - gle all the way;
49
Oh, what fun it is to ride in(a)
one - horse o - pen
53
one - horse o - pen sleigh!

Sightread one "stocking stuffer" a day while learning *Jingle Bells.*

Circle the stocking after sightreading!

("variations" for sightreading)

DAY 1

3 *on* ___?

mp Jin - gle all the, *p* jin - gle, jin - gle, jin - gle all the way.

1 *on* ___?

DAY 2

5 *on* ___?

5 1

mf Oh, what fun it is to ride in (a) one - horse o - pen sleigh!

5 *on* ___?

1 5

DAY 3

5 *on* ___?

mf One - horse o - pen, one - horse o - pen sleigh.

1 3 5

DAY 4

5 *on* ___?

1 *on* ___?

f Jin - gle bells, *p* jin - gle bells, *f* jin - gle all the way.

1 5

DAY 5

Can you sing page 17 of *Jingle Bells* without playing the piano?

Christmas Music Calendar

Complete the music calendar for each day of December.

DEC. 1

♩ + 𝅗𝅥. =

___beats

DEC. 2

Shade the key a **3rd** higher than **C**.

DEC. 3

Draw a **treble clef** on the ornament.

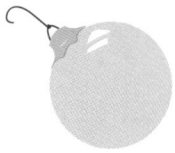

DEC. 4

Draw a **double bar line** at the end of the sleigh.

DEC. 5

Number Santa's fingers.

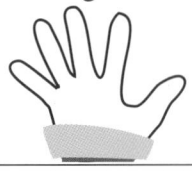

DEC. 6

Name the stars.

___ ___ ___ ___

DEC. 7

Draw a **bass clef** on Santa's beard.

DEC. 8

𝅗𝅥. 𝅗𝅥. =

___ beats

DEC. 9

Draw a **quarter rest** inside the wreath.

DEC. 10

Write your favorite **time signature**.

DEC. 11

Would prancing reindeer hooves be **staccato** or **legato**? *(circle one)*

DEC. 12

How would you rather ice skate? **legato** or **staccato**? *(circle one)*

DEC. 13

Draw a **sharp** on the tree.

DEC. 14

Write the dynamic mark for **loud** sleigh bells.

DEC. 15

Write the note names for these Christmas stars.

___ ___

DEC. 16

C up to **F** is the interval of a:
2nd 3rd 4th 5th
(circle one)

DEC. 17

How many beats are in a measure for *Jingle Bells*?

___ beats

DEC. 18

Write the dynamic mark for **soft**, fluffy snowflakes.

DEC. 19

Draw a **flat** on the present.

DEC. 20

F down to **D** is the interval of a:
2nd 3rd 4th 5th
(circle one)

DEC. 21

In **C** position,
what note is the **tonic**? ___
the **dominant**? ___

DEC. 22

Write the note names for these Christmas stars.

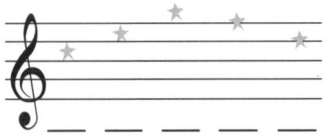

___ ___ ___ ___ ___

DEC. 23

How many **E**'s (for elves) are on your piano?

___ **E**'s

DEC. 24

Christmas Eve!

Put the dynamic marks in order, from softest to loudest.

mf f p mp

☐ ☐ ☐ ☐

DEC. 25

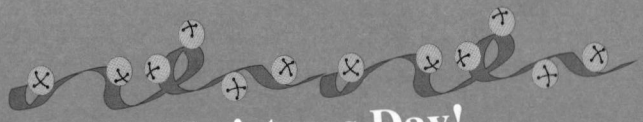

Christmas Day!

Play your favorite Christmas songs!